The Little Pine Tree

Mark Labriola

ISBN 979-8-88685-033-8 (paperback)
ISBN 979-8-88685-035-2 (hardcover)
ISBN 979-8-88685-034-5 (digital)

Christian Faith Publishing
832 Park Avenue
Meadville, PA 16335
www.christianfaithpublishing.com

Printed in the United States of America

I would like to dedicate this story to my kind wife, Janet, the love of my life, as well as my inspiration and devoted fan, and also to my Lord and Savior, Jesus Christ, who has chosen the foolish things of the world to confound the wise and who has chosen the weak things of the world to confound the things that are mighty.

One day, a brisk wind was blowing through the forest, and one special little pine seed was caught by a gust and blown far away from all the other trees. This made the little seed sad. Then worst of all, autumn turned into winter, and snow covered the little pine seed. It was dark and cold, which made him even sadder.

But quickly, winter turned to spring, and the warm sun caused the snow to melt. This fed the little pine seed, and his roots sunk deep into the fertile patch of soil. Soon, the warm sun came out and gave the little pine seed life.

It wasn't long before the little seed poked its first branch out of the ground and became a little tree. Now he knew that one day, he would have a wonderful purpose and be a blessing to mankind just like all the other trees. Many seasons passed with warm sun, soaking rain, and melting snow feeding the little pine tree, but he only grew a few inches each year.

I must be patient, thought the little pine tree, hoping all the time that a carpenter would finally discover him. But the little pine tree wasn't very tall and way too far from all the other trees, so the carpenters never saw him.

Then one day, to his surprise, a little boy came to the forest with his dad, a local carpenter. He was a sweet boy and spent all his time with the little pine tree.

I love having a friend, thought the little pine tree. *Surely, this boy will show me to the carpenter! But if not, at least, I have a friend.*

Now the little pine tree wasn't lonely anymore. The carpenter's boy would come and sit with him. He was a kind and gentle boy, and this made the little pine tree happy. They were friends, and that was special.

The bunnies, raccoons, and songbirds would all come and play with the boy and the little pine tree too. Sometimes, the little boy would kneel on the ground and call for someone named Abba. *Maybe the carpenter will hear him*, thought the little pine tree. *Maybe the carpenter will come for me*. But he never did. The little pine tree could only wait. But while he waited, he grew, and he grew.

As time passed and the little boy got older, the little pine tree lost all hope of ever being found by the carpenter; alas, it still wasn't time. For a while, the boy came often then less and less until eventually, he never came back at all.

After many years, the little pine tree grew very tall. The little pine tree felt so alone since the little boy had long since stopped coming. He wished when he was a seed that he hadn't blown so far from all the other trees in the forest. The little pine tree was afraid that he would never be found, never have a purpose, and never ever be a blessing to mankind.

Then one spring day, there was a noise in the forest. It was soldiers. *Why are they here?* the little pine tree thought. Soon, they found the little pine tree. *How exciting! I will finally have a purpose*, thought the little pine tree.

The soldiers began chopping at the little pine tree's trunk until it hit the ground with a loud thump. They lifted it onto a cart and began to march into town.

It was a long bumpy ride. Then at last, they arrived. The soldiers lifted the little pine tree and put him on a long table. *I wonder what I will become. Will they make me into a table or a chair or a bed?* The little pine tree was so happy now.

The soldiers brought in a huge saw. They cut, and they cut. *Finally, I have a purpose and will be a blessing to mankind.* But as he lay there on the table, he wondered, *What have they done with me? I've never seen anything like this before. What possibly could I be used for now?* It was hard for him to see, but the soldiers had cut the little pine tree into a tall pine cross.

The soldiers put the little pine tree back on the cart, took him to town, and leaned him against a wall outside the courtyard.

As the little pine tree cross rested against the wall, he heard crowds of people yelling. The little pine tree could see on the platform in the courtyard a solitary man, lonesome just like he had been in the forest for all those years.

But why did he look so familiar? But wait, wait, and then he remembered. *The carpenter's boy! The little boy who talked to me in the forest who promised that one day, I would have a great purpose and be a blessing to mankind.* It *was* the carpenter's boy. But he had grown and was now a full-grown man.

To the little pine tree's astonishment, the carpenter's boy was led out of the courtyard and was made to carry the little pine tree cross. He was very weak. *Oh no, this cannot be my purpose*, thought the little pine tree.

When they reached the hilltop, the soldiers nailed the carpenter's boy to the little pine tree cross. The little pine tree never imagined that he would have such a dreadful purpose. Oh, how he wished that a carpenter had found him in the forest instead.

Now I will never be a blessing to mankind. This is not what I wanted to be, nothing at all like this! cried the little pine tree.

Three days had passed since the carpenter's boy was taken down from the little pine tree cross. *How sad*, thought the little pine tree. *Why did he promise that I would have a wonderful purpose? It was such a horrible thing they did.* Once again, the little pine tree was set apart from all the other trees, but this time as a tall pine cross on a deserted hill.

On that third morning as the sun began to rise, the little pine tree saw someone approaching. *Who could this be?* thought the little pine tree. The person was remarkably beautiful, and he even seemed to glow.

"Hello, friend, my name is Jesus. Do you remember me?"

"I think so. Were you the little boy who sat with me in the forest?" the little pine tree asked.

"Yes," said Jesus. "When I was a boy, I always knew that one day, you would be my cross. That is why you were set apart from all the other trees."

"But I was used for such a dreadful purpose," said the little pine tree.

"Yes, you were, but it's because my Father and I love mankind so much. It was the only way to pay for their sin."

"But now you're alive!" the little pine tree exclaimed.

"Yes, I am alive," Jesus replied.

"I am the Son of God, and I rose from the grave so that whoever believes in me will never die but live with me forever in *heaven*. Yes, little pine tree, your purpose was painful, but as you can see, you have become the most wonderful of all the trees. Because you served as my cross, you were given the highest purpose and will forever be the *greatest* blessing to mankind, *now and for all time*!

But God forbid that I should glory,
save in the cross of our Lord Jesus
Christ. (Galatians 6:14 KJV)

ABOUT THE AUTHOR

Mark currently lives just off Anna Maria Island, Florida, with his wife, Jan, and their bulldog, Brick. This story was written to reach the hearts of parents and children for Jesus Christ.